The Gu

GW01079935

The Guide was originally produced by the Peddars   's
inaugural meeting in Swaffham on 14th Novemb   n
objectives:-

1. To press for official designation and completion of the footpath.
2. To promote and publicise the use of the route and its amenities for the benefit of walkers and cyclists.
3. To promote a body of informed opinion that will improve the enjoyment and knowledge of Peddars Way.

As these original objectives appeared to have been achieved and maintenance of the Guide and Accommodation list seemed to be the remaining work, the Peddars Way Association was wound-up at a meeting of members at Dereham on 23rd March 1996, it was agreed that all the assets of the Association should be transferred to the Norfolk Area of the Ramblers' Association, which would continue to edit, publish and distribute the guide book.

The guide is intended to help you plan a holiday or just a day's walk on part of the track and has been kept as simple and inexpensive as possible. The route is described by means of twelve maps, the first seven of which should be read from bottom to top, and the last five from top to bottom. The maps are not fully to scale, but an indication of distance is shown on each sheet. Additional text is there to help you through the trickier sections. There is a separate list to help with accommodation, public transport and places of interest.

If you discover anything needing correction or additional information that would improve the guide, we would like to hear from you, the Guide Editor's address is below.

The Ordnance Survey Landranger maps (1:50,000) numbers 144, 132, 133 and 134 are recommended for the extra detail and information they contain. Even more detail is in the new Explorer maps (1:25000) 229, 236, 250, 251, 252 and Outdoor Leisure map 40.

GUIDE EDITOR   Ian Mitchell
                5, Montcalm Road, Norwich, NR1 4HX   Telephone 01603 622539
DISTRIBUTION Sheila Smith, Caldcleugh, Old Buckenham, E-mail: sheilasmith@clara.co.uk
                Attleborough, Norfolk, NR17 1RU   Telephone 01953 861094

ACKNOWLEDGEMENTS:

Original maps and route descriptions by Alan & Penny Jenyon.
Ian Smith & Colin Hills.
Accommodation list by Ian Mitchell, John Kent, Derek Goddard & Sheila Smith
Computer layout by Sheila Smith.

Published by: The Ramblers Association, Norfolk Area

37th Edition. Revised and reprinted regularly. September, 2005

Introduction

A guide to a route of 149 miles (239 kilometres), showing the surprising variety of Norfolk scenery from Knettishall Heath on the Suffolk border to Great Yarmouth.

The **PEDDARS WAY** is an ancient track, mainly Roman in the form in which we see today, but probably pre-Roman in origin. The original route may have run from Colchester to Lincolnshire, with a ferry or ford over the Wash. Peddars Way certainly contributed to the downfall of Queen Boadicea and the Iceni tribes. The surviving part of the route stretches from Knettishall Heath near Thetford in the south, to the coast at Holme. The Secretary of State for the Environment approved the Countryside Commission's proposals in Oct.1982 for a long distance route of 93 miles (149kms) to be known as **THE PEDDARS WAY and NORFOLK COAST PATH.**

THE FOOTPATH WAS OFFICIALLY OPENED on JULY 8th 1986 by

HRH. PRINCE CHARLES.

The **WEAVERS WAY** footpath, from Cromer to Gt. Yarmouth, devised by Norfolk County Council has been included in this guide as a continuation of the long distance path and adding another 56 miles (90kms).

A further route called the **ANGLES WAY** has been created by Norfolk & Suffolk County Councils, to link the Weavers Way at Yarmouth to the Peddars Way at Knettishall Heath, thus creating a circular route of 226 miles (362kms).

TABLE OF DISTANCES	miles	kilometres
PEDDARS WAY	47	75
NORFOLK COAST PATH	46	74
Long Distance Path Total	93	149
WEAVERS WAY	56	90
Total covered in Guide	149	239
ANGLES WAY	77	123
Total "Round Norfolk"	226	362

ICENI WAY - A walk from Knettishall Heath via Thetford & Brandon along the banks of the Little & Great Ouse to Kings Lynn and via Sandringham to Hunstanton. This includes a 15mile (24kms) off-road route between Knettishall Heath and Thetford. The Iceni Way and Peddars Way together can provide a 130 mile (210 km) circuit with easier transport links.

Guides & accommodation lists for the **Angles Way** and the **Iceni Way** are available from Ramblers Association, Sheila Smith, Caldcleugh, Cake Street, Old Buckenham, Attleborough, NR17 1RU. They each cost £3.00, including post and packing.

A cloth badge, to commemorate your journey along the Peddars Way and Norfolk Coast Path, is available in return for your comments. For details contact: -
The National Trail Office, The Old Courthouse, Baron's Close, Fakenham, Norfolk, NR21 8BE
Email: nationaltrail@norfolk.gov.uk. Tel: 01328 850530

Peddars Way & Norfolk Coast Path

Symbols used on maps

Major roads	Railway	Church	S	Shop

Major roads
Minor roads
Tracks
Footpaths

Railway
Disused Railway
River and Bridge
Sea Embankment

Church
Windmill/windpump
Youth Hostel
C Camping
BK Bunk Barn

S Shop
PH Public House
R Refreshments
PC Toilets
P Car park

Until reaching point 8 the maps should be read from the bottom working upwards.

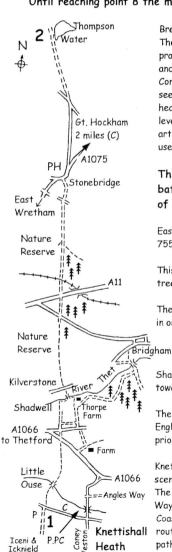

Breckland is the unique region of heathland crossed by Peddars Way. The soil is sandy, dry and infertile, partly due to the Neolithic farming practice of 'slash and burn', crops are prone to drought in a dry summer and much of the area has been planted with conifers by the Forestry Commission. Something of the original character of the area can be seen approaching Thompson Water with Scots pine scattered on open heath. There are several Breckland 'meres' which have higher water levels in summer than in winter! Thompson Water, however, is an artificial lake dug out in the 19th century and more recently has been used for trout farming.

This section of the route passes through the Stanford battle training area. Do not stray from the path because of the danger from unexploded shells.

East Wretham Heath, Norfolk Wildlife Trust Reserve: T. 01842 755010.

This section of Peddars Way is at its finest in Spring when the May trees are in bloom.

There is a nature reserve here maintained by the Nature Conservancy in order to preserve some of the traditional Breckland.

Shadwell is named after Chad's well, a shrine for pilgrims. The church tower has been buttressed for over 600 years but still stands strong.

Thetford, meaning 'the people's ford' was the capital of Anglo-Saxon England in King Canute's time. Castle Hill earthworks, 800 year old priory and Ancient House Museum (archaeology) open daily.

Knettishall Heath Country Park preserves some traditional Breckland scenery and is a centre for serious ramblers and gentle strollers. The Angles Way is a 78 mile route to Great Yarmouth, the Icknield Way connects with The Ridgeway and the Iceni Way joins the Norfolk Coastal Path at Hunstanton following an 80 mile Breck and Fenland route around south and west Norfolk. There are also numerous footpaths across the Heath for short rambles.

(9 miles [15km] approx. 1-2)

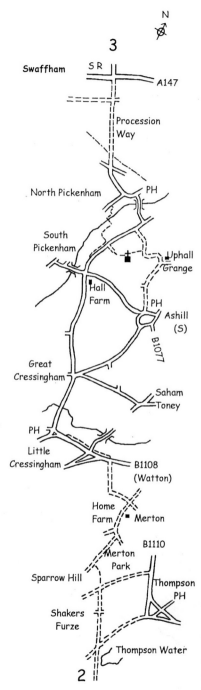

N

3

Swaffham S R

A147

Procession
Way

North Pickenham   PH

South
Pickenham

Uphall
Grange

Hall
Farm   PH

Ashill
(S)

B1077

Great
Cressingham

Saham
Toney

PH

Little
Cressingham   B1108
(Watton)

Home
Farm   Merton

B1110

Merton
Park

Sparrow Hill

Thompson
PH

Shakers
Furze

Thompson Water

2

(13 miles [21km] approx. 2-3)

Swaffham is an old market town with a lively Saturday market: auctions of bric-a-brac, farm produce, cars and livestock. The village sign recalls the legend of the pedlar of Swaffham. The fine 15th century church has a splendid double hammer-beam roof, with 150 angels carved 500 years ago.

Access to the Peddars Way from the southeast edge of Swaffham is off the North Pickenham Road by a steep vehicle track eastward, indicated by a metal signpost. Procession Way is reached after one mile along this track

Procession Way derives its name from the regular religious processions which used it in medieval times.

On the hill towards Uphall Grange is the recently restored St. Mary's Church, Houghton-on-the-Hill, where 10th or 11th century wall paintings were found.

South Pickenham Hall to your left is a fine example of a country house built in the neo-Georgian style in 1902 - 05. There is a round tower church nearby.

Great Cressingham is an old village with thatched cottages and a fine 14th century church, with some fine brasses and memories of Cromwell's time.

Watton is an old town with a Norman church and 14th century belfry. Nearby is Wayland Wood or 'wailing wood' - the place of the legend 'Babes in the Wood'.

North of Home Farm a bridleway leading straight on reaches B1108 on the western edge of Watton, from there a bridleway and road leads to Saham Toney.

Merton, originally 'mere town', has Roman connections. It has a fine 13th century church.

On reaching Sparrow Hill go on northwards in the fenced section at the edge of the battle area. This joins a track which enters Merton Park in which you continue due north, finally coming out onto the track which passes Home Farm.

The village of Thompson existed before the conquest and the church is one the best examples to be found in Norfolk of the early decorated period - 14th century.

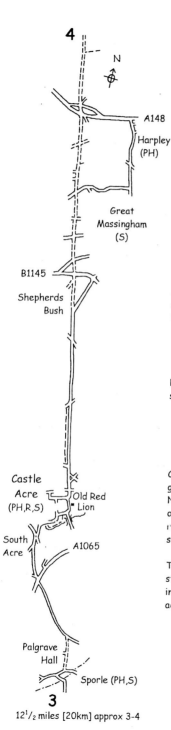

4

N

A148

Harpley
(PH)

Great
Massingham
(S)

B1145

Shepherds
Bush

Castle
Acre
(PH,R,S)

Old Red
Lion

South
Acre

A1065

Palgrave
Hall

Sporle (PH,S)

3

12½ miles [20km] approx 3-4

Several good examples of tumuli - ancient burial mounds - can be seen on this stretch of the route.

Great Massingham is noted for the size of the village pond. Nearby is a fine 14th century church with a pinnacled tower and remains of an 11th century priory.

Shepherds Bush is one of the highest points on the Norfolk stretch of the Peddars Way. Another Roman road, from Brisley to King's Lynn, may have crossed the route about here.

Notice the change in scenery from the infertile Breckland in the south to the highly cultivated rolling hills of west Norfolk.

Castle Acre has Roman, Saxon and Norman connections. The tall gateway opening onto the village green was a gate of the castle in Norman times. The castle hill is on the site of the Roman camp, one of the biggest East Anglian fortresses of the day. A Roman road, from Denver to Smallburgh once crossed west to east just south of the town.

The Norman Priory can be seen from the road by South Acre. It stands next to the river which the monks used to supply fishponds in the priory grounds. The buildings and foundations cover 36 acres. Access is from the street west of the church.

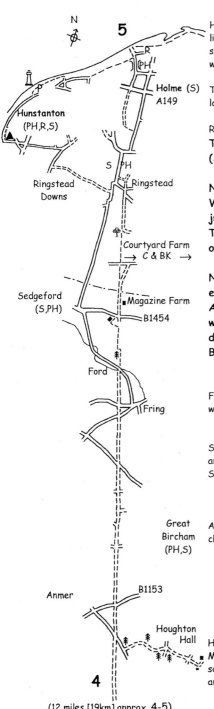

N

5

Hunstanton its heyday in the Victorian railway era – the line is now closed. On clear evenings you can watch the sun setting over the sea. The cliffs are striped red and white with carrstone and chalk and Fulmars breed here.

The carrstone is quarried locally and can be seen in many local buildings, although it is not particularly durable.

Ringstead Downs is a chalkland valley, unusual in Norfolk. **This is a quick way into Hunstanton if needed. (3 miles or 5km.)**

North of the disused railway, follow Peddars Way across the field or use the farm track just to the east - both are rights of way. The Peddars Way continues along the west side of the hedge, up the hill towards Ringstead.

North of the Fring to Sedgeford Road, stay east of the hedge until you reach a small wood. A little further on is a sign taking you to the west side of the hedge. Follow signs on a diversion around a field as you approach the B1454.

Fring has a 14th century church with its belfry windows still intact.

Sandringham (off the route) house, gardens, museum and nature trail. Open Sunday to Thursday, April to September - but closed on special occasions.

Anmer, a village on the Sandringham estate, with a fine church and 16th century Hall.

Houghton Hall built by Sir Robert Walpole, first Prime Minister of England. There is a large collection of model soldiers. Open Easter to September, Sundays, Thursdays and Bank holidays. 2.30 - 5.30 pm. (T. 01485 528569)

(12 miles [19km] approx. 4-5)

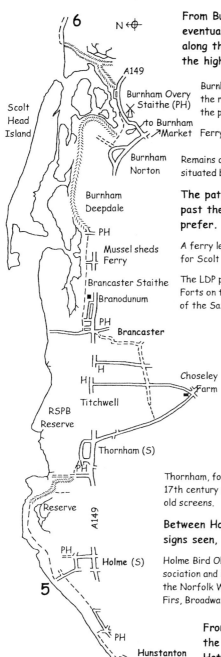

From Burnham Overy Staithe go along the sea bank, eventually reaching the beach. The right of way is along the beach. In May, June and July walk below the high tide line to avoid nesting terns.

Burnham Thorpe (two miles inland) - Nelson's birthplace in the rectory has been demolished. A plaque on a wall marks the place.

Ferry runs from the Staithe to Scolt Head in summer months.

Remains of St. Mary's Carmelite Friary, founded 1241, are situated between Burnham Market and Burnham Overy Town.

The path from the mussel sheds follows the bank top past the houses, you may walk on the marsh if you prefer.

A ferry leaves from Brancaster Staithe in the summer months for Scolt Head National Reserve (tern colonies).

The LDP passes Branodunum the site of one of three Roman Forts on the Norfolk coast. Dalmatian cavalry under "The Count of the Saxon Shore" dealt with invaders from the Continent.

Between Thornham and Brancaster there is no safe route to the seaward side of the A149, nor is there a footpath beside the main road for those wishing to visit the RSPB Reserve, or who have accommodation in Titchwell. To avoid this busy road it is necessary to divert inland nearly as far as Choseley Farm, but the views are out-standing.

Thornham, formerly famous for its forge, is worth visiting for its 17th century manor house and 14th century church with 500 year old screens.

Between Holme and Thornham observe any diversion signs seen, as the path is subject to erosion.

Holme Bird Observatory is run by the Norfolk Ornithologists' Association and is famous for sightings of migratory birds. Nearby is the Norfolk Wildlife Trust reserve and nature trail. Details: The Firs, Broadwater Road, Holme. Tel: 01485 552240

From Hunstanton go to the lighthouse then along the cliff footpath and behind the le Strange Hotel, turn inland, then after a short way go northeast again along links road, past the club house and skirt south side of golf links to reach Holme via the beach road.

(19 miles [30km] approx. Hunstanton-6)

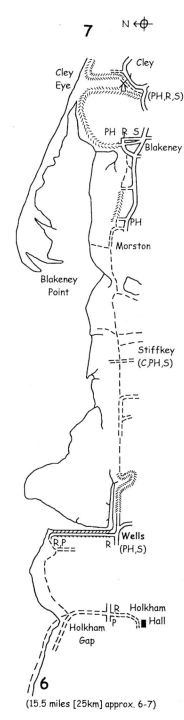

7 N ←⊕

Cley Eye

Cley

(PH,R,S)

PH R S/L

Blakeney

PH

Morston

Blakeney Point

Stiffkey
(C,PH,S)

Wells
(PH,S)

R.P   R

JLR   Holkham
P   ■ Hall

Holkham
Gap

6

(15.5 miles [25km] approx. 6-7)

Glandford Shell Museum (2 miles south from Cley), by the Church - a world-wide collection. Also Tapestry of the Norfolk coast. Open from March to October. Tuesday to Saturday and Bank holidays. 10 - 12.30, 2 - 4.30. GR: 044414.

From Blakeney, go seawards on the sea wall and cross the River Glaven at the sluice next to A149. Continue to Cley High Street. Turn left along the busy street, but soon turn left to the sea wall and turn right to Cley Mill. Pass to the right of the mill and follow the sea bank to the coastguard station at Cley Eye.

Blakeney used to be a great seaport, provisioning the tall ships used in the crusades. Now the harbour is silted up, the only boats are small pleasure craft and a few passenger ferries making trips to view the seals and land at Blakeney Point in the summer. Ferry also from Morston to Blakeney Point in the summer months.

Saltmarshes are a characteristic of this part of the coast and are a wintering and breeding area for birds. Most of this coast has been purchased by conservation bodies, mainly the National Trust. The plants are specially adapted to withstand occasional inundation by seawater. One of these plants provides the local delicacy "samphire".

Stiffkey famous for its cockles (Stewkey Blues) which are commemorated on the village sign.

Be careful if you go seawards over the marsh and sandflats. It is easy to lose your way and be cut-off by a rising tide.

Wells is the only port left on the North Norfolk coast with a usable harbour and is occasionally used for the movement of grain and fertilizer. A number of fishing and pleasure craft moor here.

Holkham Hall the 18th century home of the Earls of Leicester. (Coke of Norfolk became famous for his Norfolk Rotation and other pioneering agricultural methods). Hall (tapestries and pictures) and Bygones Museum open 1 - 5 pm Sunday - Thursday, June to September and 11.30 - 5pm Sunday and Monday Easter, Spring and Summer Bank holidays. Normally there is all year access to the park walks (fallow deer and bird life).

Holkham pines planted to stop the sand dunes from moving inland, so that the marshes could be reclaimed.

Go along the beach until you reach the board walk at Holkham Gap, then go inland of the woods and turn east-wards along the track between the woods and the marsh. Go onto the top of the sea bank for the approach to Wells.

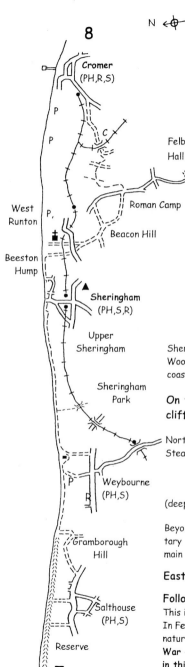

The Cromer Ridge, which is the high ground inland of the town is evidence of glaciation during the ice ages.

Cromer is famous for crab fishing. Sea defences attempt to control the erosion of the cliffs, a problem on this part of the coast. The church tower is the highest in Norfolk after Norwich Cathedral.

Felbrigg Hall a 17th century house with original 18th century furniture. Walled garden, tea shop. National Trust, open April to October. Saturday to Wednesday 1 pm - 5pm

Leave Sheringham by the sea-front and take the path over Beeston Hump along the cliff. Turn right, following the left edge of a field, over the level crossing and across the main road. Go past Beeston Hall and after a sharp turn left at the bottom of the hill, fork right and go up towards Beacon Hill and Roman Camp. Go over the road and bear left into a footpath in front of a gate. Go down through the wood as far as the Camping Club site, then turn right onto a path, go over Abbs Common and into a green lane. Continue under the railway bridge to reach Cromer.

Sheringham Park is known for its exotic plants and Rhododendron Woods. Grounds open all the year (NT), there is a fine view of the coast from the Gazebo.

On the cliff edge route into Sheringham be wary of the cliffs and golfers.

North Norfolk Railway, Sheringham - Weybourne - High Kelling. Steam trains on summer weekends and bank holidays.

'He that would olde Englande win
Should at Weybourne Hope begin.'
(deep water close to the shore would have been of help to an invasion).

Beyond the redundant radar station the sight and sound of old military vehicles comes from the Muckleburgh Collection. Entrance on main road GR: 105428.

East of Gramborough hill the walking becomes easier.

Follow the shingle bank, on top or either side.
This is remounded mechanically, possibly several times every winter. In February 1996 it was washed over and the salt water flooded the nature reserve. **Mines placed on the beach during the 1939-45 War occasionally reappear, keep a lookout.** Bathing is not safe in this area anyway.

Norfolk Wildlife Trust Information Centre with an exhibition about the North Norfolk Coast is the thatched cottage just east of Cley.

(12 miles [19km] approx. 7- Cromer)

Weavers Way

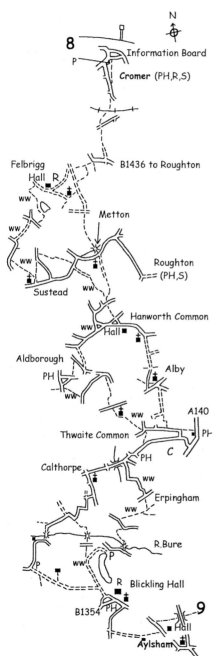

You may now set off on the Weavers Way which is a route developed and published by the Norfolk County Council. It is 56 miles from Cromer to Great Yarmouth. The route was revised in 1997.

The following maps are based on the information in a leaflet, available from: Planning & Transportation, County Hall, Martineau Lane, Norwich, NR1 2DH and local tourist information centres.

The current route is waymarked with disks on posts, and is shown with "WW" on this map. The previous route is also shown here as it appears on the Explorer Map, published early in 1997.

Eastern Norfolk has a concentration of round tower churches. There are very few in the country outside Norfolk and Suffolk. W.J. Goode, in his book 'Round Tower Churches of South East England' argues that the construction of many of them is Saxon, dating from as early as 800 AD.

Round tower - St. Peter & St. Paul, Sustead.

St Bartholomew's Church at Hanworth dates from the 14th - 15th century and has fine medieval workmanship.

Round tower – All Saints Church, Thwaite.

Thwaite common, an area of semi-natural grassland which, although privately owned, has rights of pasture over it.

St Margaret's Church, Calthorpe, mainly dates from the 13th century.

Blickling Hall was built 1616-27. One of the most impressive Jacobean houses in England, now owned by the National Trust. The house is open during the season: April to October 1pm - 4.30pm Wednesday to Sunday plus Bank Holiday Mondays. Also Tuesdays in August. Garden as above from 10.30 am. The path around the lake is open at any time.

St. Andrews Church, Blickling, has a number of brasses.

(15 miles [24km] approx. 8—9]

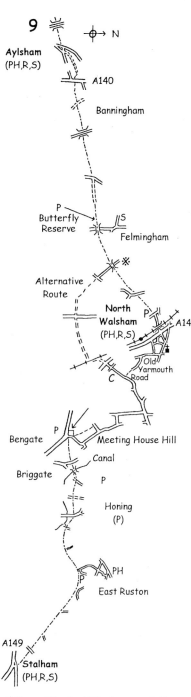

9
Aylsham
(PH,R,S)

N

A140

Banningham

P
Butterfly
Reserve

S
Felmingham

Alternative
Route

North
Walsham
(PH,R,S)

A149

Old
Yarmouth
Road

C

Bengate

P
Meeting House Hill

Canal

Briggate

P

Honing
(P)

PH
P

East Ruston

A149
Stalham
(PH,R,S)

10   (14 miles [23km] approx. 9-10

Aylsham was an important medieval centre for the manufacture of fine linen cloth called Aylsham Webb. It is still a thriving market town.

Most of the route of this map follows the disused track of the former Midland and Great Northern railway line from King's Lynn to Great Yarmouth. (the sections not following the track are well signposted.

The line was closed in 1959 and since then a pleasing variety of trees, shrubs and wildflowers have colonised the route making a very attractive path and bridleway.

Those wishing to avoid North Walsham may use the signposted official diversion to Meeting House Hill.

This route crosses a battlefield of 1381 during the Peasants Revolt.

North Walsham was another important medieval centre for the weaving industry of the area, with an important market for both wool and finished cloth. Today it is still a market town with considerable industry.

Go through the town centre past the market cross and leave by the Old Yarmouth Road, follow the footpath and go left into the minor road. At the crossroads turn right into Holgate Lane then go first left, first right, to Meeting House Hill.

Turn right to a footpath then left across the field back to the disused railway just before the bypass.

The village of Worstead, a few miles off the route, from Bengate, gave its name to worstead cloth. This village was extremely wealthy when the wool industry was at its height, as shown by the size of the church. Today it is a small though attractive village.

North Walsham and Dilham Canal was built in the early 19th century to bring coal into North Walsham and goods out, but never a commercial success.

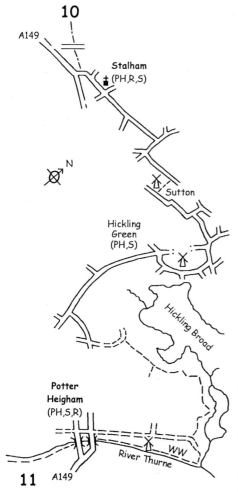

10

A149

Stalham
(PH,R,S)

N

Sutton

Hickling
Green
(PH,S)

Hickling Broad

Potter
Heigham
(PH,S,R)

WW
River Thurne

11   A149

(10 miles [16km] approx. 10-11)

The final section of The Weavers' Way from Stalham to Great Yarmouth is a further 27 miles (43km).

The route includes extensive Broadland riverside stretches with wide views over open valley land and marshes. There is a striking contrast between the traditional undrained marshland around Hickling Broad and the newly drained agricultural land of the lower Bure and Yare. Many old windpumps formerly used for drainage are notable landmarks.

Stalham, now a holiday centre on the edge of the Broads, has long been a centre for the surrounding countryside: wherries plied between here and Great Yarmouth.

The Way first follows minor country roads but takes a footpath past Sutton Windmill — the tallest surviving mill in the country with all machinery still in place.

Hickling Broad national nature reserve covers 1200 acres (485 hectares), including all Hickling Broad and Heigham Sound. Surrounded by reed beds and fen, it is an important habitat for breeding and over-wintering birds. **Please take extra care to protect the wildlife.**

From the nature reserve entrance to Acle most of the way is along river banks. It skirts the south edge of Hickling Broad and side of Heigham Sound. South of Potter Heigham it follows the Thurne and Bure.

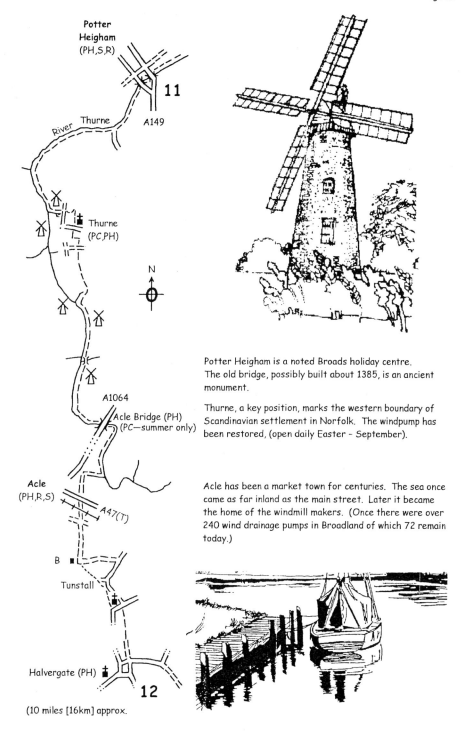

Potter Heigham (PH,S,R)

11

River Thurne A149

Thurne (PC,PH)

N

A1064

Acle Bridge (PH) (PC—summer only)

Acle (PH,R,S) A47(T)

B

Tunstall

Halvergate (PH)

12

Potter Heigham is a noted Broads holiday centre. The old bridge, possibly built about 1385, is an ancient monument.

Thurne, a key position, marks the western boundary of Scandinavian settlement in Norfolk. The windpump has been restored, (open daily Easter – September).

Acle has been a market town for centuries. The sea once came as far inland as the main street. Later it became the home of the windmill makers. (Once there were over 240 wind drainage pumps in Broadland of which 72 remain today.)

(10 miles [16km] approx.

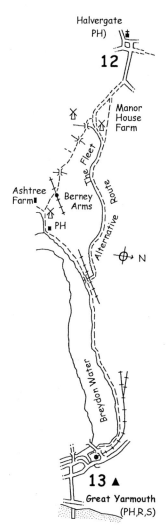

Halvergate
PH)

12

Manor
House
Farm

the Fleet

Ashtree
Farm

Berney
Arms

PH

Alternative Route

N

Breydon Water

13 ▲

Great Yarmouth
(PH,R,S)

(7 miles [11km] approx. 12-13)

The way now crosses low-lying farmland and grazing marshes, some of the largest and most important in the country. Paths often remain boggy till May – boots advised.

The path follows the old marsh road to Manor House Farm, then across the marshes to the Berney Arms to join the path along Breydon Wall and Breydon Sluice. (Please close gates.)

Berney Arms windpump is an ancient monument dating from 1870 (open April–September but times vary).

Breydon Water, a local nature reserve, is important for migrating birds especially waders and wildfowl. Boats raised on stilts are observation huts.

The way follows the flood wall on the north Bank of Breydon Water to Great Yarmouth. Pass Vauxhall Station, continue via North Quay and Market Place to the Tourist Information Centre near Britannia Pier.

Great Yarmouth was built on a sandbar that shifted many times and led to a constant medieval battle to keep the harbour open. The town developed as a fishing port, becoming a popular holiday resort in the 19th century. The old commercial centre faces the harbour and the "new" town of hotels, boarding houses and entertainments faces the sea.

Transport

TRAINS serving the area are run by Anglia Railways, Central Trains and WAGN. These stations may be useful for getting into the area: On the route: Sheringham, Cromer, North Walsham, Acle, Berney Arms, Great Yarmouth. Others: King's Lynn, Thetford, Bury St. Edmunds, Diss, Norwich. . Information on times and fares from staffed stations and National Rail Enquiries: 08457 48 49 50

BUSES Enquiries to Traveline 0870 608 2608 daily, 8.00 - 20.00. www.traveline.org.uk

Bus Information Centre, Castle Meadow, Norwich, Monday- Saturday 8.30 - 17.00

The following regular all year service routes may be useful:

King's Lynn—Swaffham—Norwich

King's Lynn—Massingham—Fakenham—Wells

King's Lynn—Fakenham—Sheringham—Cromer

Norwich—Aylsham—Cromer—Sheringham

Norwich—Acle—Great Yarmouth

Watton—Dereham—Norwich—Yarmouth—Lowestoft

Watton—Thetford (Post-bus)

King's Lynn—Hunstanton (at least hourly)

King's Lynn—Swaffham—Watton—Attleborough—Diss

Sheringham—Wells—Hunstanton

Norwich—North Walsham

Norwich—Fakenham—(Wells on Sunday)

Norwich—Wymondham—Attleborough—Watton—Ashill

Express Bus services between Thetford and Norwich do not stop anywhere near the Peddars Way crossing of the A11.

Coastal Bus Service 36 run by Norfolk Green (T. 01553 776980) daily throughout the year between Hunstanton and Sheringham. Even on winter Sundays there are 3 buses each way and the coast path could be walked in short lengths using this service from a several night stopover. There are connecting services to King's Lynn and Cromer or Norwich.

KNETTISHALL HEATH is 5 miles (8 kms) by direct road from Thetford railway station, about half being along the busy A1066. **There is no security for cars at Knettishall Heath and they should not be left there except during a day walk.**

Limited bus services as shown below. Alternatively use part of the Iceni Way for a 15 mile (24 km) walkers route from Thetford, or a similar distance from Diss via the Angles Way. (see page 2). Diss railway station is on main London to Norwich line.

Buses running near the southern end of Peddars Way

337/338 (not Sunday) Bury St. Edmunds - Garboldisham via Barningham & Coney Weston (2.5mls, 4km by minor road and path to Peddars Way).

191 (college days only) Early morning Diss - Thetford. Early evening Thetford - Diss, both via Home Farm, Riddlesworth (GR 959820) (1ml, 1.5km by minor road to Knettishall Heath).

192 (Mon-Fri.) Thetford - Diss via Bridgham & East Harling 1 or 2 services per day, each way.

Peddars Wayfarer, for walkers & cyclists, bus with trailer. Daily late March to end October. 2 services per day, each way, stopping at access points on Peddars Way and nearby villages. Thetford (bus & rail stations) - Knettishall Heath - Swaffham. Enquiries to 01328 850530 or www.nationaltrail.co.uk

Brecks Bus, around Thetford & Brandon, including Knettishall Heath and part of Peddars Way. Available Mon-Fri 09.00-16.00 for the journey you require (max 5 people). Book before noon, day prior to travel. Enquiries to 01842 816170 or www.brecks.org.uk

Pick up service and onward baggage delivery.

Some guesthouses, etc. (those serving the southern part of the Peddars Way include a number located at a distance from the route) are willing to pick you up from the route at the end of your day's walking and set you down again the next morning. Some will deliver your baggage to your next night's accommodation. Contact them individually to check what arrangements they are able to offer. Arrangements should always be made in advance and charges will vary. Some establishments will require a minimum two nights (or more) booking for the Pick-up Service, many probably prefer that you stay more than one night.

Accommodation

Places providing accommodation within half an hour of the route have been included unless a longer distance is specified. Please let us know of any places that do not meet a reasonable standard or have closed. We should also like to hear of places which are worth including.
An indication is given to some accommodation prices but prices should be checked at time of booking. A premium is sometimes asked for singles, possibly placing them in the next higher price band.

The following towns are known to have more accommodation than we can list, so in case of difficulty their tourist information phone numbers are given:

| Hunstanton | 01485 532610 | Wells | 0870 225 4857 | Sheringham | 0870 225 4854 |
| Cromer | 0870 225 4853 | Swaffham | 01760 722255 | Great Yarmouth | 01493 846345 |

The following abbreviations have been used:

B	Bank/Building Society	S	Shop (Early closing Wednesday if not stated)	£	to £18 a night
R	Refreshments/Meals	C	Campsite or possible camping, eg garden of a pub	£+	£18 to £23
G	Guest House	EM	Evening meal (at guest house always by booking)	£++	£23 to £26
Y	Hostel YHA or other	H	Hotel D Double room	T. Telephone	£+++	£26 to £30
PH	Public House	I	Inn T Twin room	F. Fax	£++++	£30 or over
BB	Bed & Breakfast	BK	Bunk Barn S Single room	Std Telephone area code	
S/n	No smoking	PC	Toilets F Family room	GR: Grid reference	
S/r	Smoking restrictions	L	Lunch E Evening	Cyc Secure place for cycles	
Rstr.	Restaurant	B/m	Bar meals	D/f Drying facilities	
V	Vegetarian menu available	P/l	Packed lunches by arrangement	Dgs Dogs by arrangement	
P/u	Pick up service		Charges will vary. **Always** confirm		
B/d	Onward baggage delivery	}	arrangements in advance.		
#	Location only suitable if combined with pick up service or similar.				

Establishments open throughout the year (possibly excluding Xmas and New Year) unless otherwise stated.

Postal towns should not be assumed to have any geographical relevance.

Knettishall Heath Std 01953   For access to Knettishall Heath please see details on previous page.
Car Parking – GR:944807 and GR:956807, but **No Security.**

C   GR:955807. Please inform Country Park Warden. (T.688265)

PC   No Shop. Information Office Open At Weekends. GR:955807

Coney Weston, (Bury St. Edmunds) Std 01359 2 miles (4kms) by Lane S.E. of Country Park

PH C   Swan, Thetford Road, IP31 1DN. T.221295. jack.stimpson@btinternet.com Snacks. Tent space.

BB   Barbara Clarke, Lundy Cottage, Thetford Rd, IP31 1DN. T.221906 peterclarke1001@hotmail.com
        BB £++ T1.   V, P/l, S/n, D/f, Cyc, P/u, B/d

Barningham, (Bury St. Edmunds) Std 01359 3.5 miles (5kms) by Lane S.E. of Country Park

PH R S   Royal George – meals. Village store.

Barnham (Thetford) Std 01842 5 miles (8kms) via **Iceni Way,** see page 2 to Euston, then by minor road.

BB   Mrs. M. Heading, East Farm, Euston Road. IP24 2PB. T.890231. F.890457. BB £++ /£+++
        D1, T1.   P/l, S/n, D/f, Cyc. P/u,

PH   Grafton Arms – meals

Garboldisham (Diss) Std 01953 4 miles (6.5kms) via **Angles Way** (see page 2.)

BB   Ingleneuk Lodge, Hopton Road, IP22 2RQ. T.681541. F.681138. www.ingleneuk-lodge.co.uk
        BB £++++ D2, T2, S1. V, P/l, S/r, D/f, Cyc, P/u, B/d Res. license. E B/m by arrangement.

Taxi   Rod Middleton T.681541. rod@rodmid.freewire.co.uk Any length of journey. Advance booking.

East Harling (Norwich) Std 01953. 5 mls (8kms) road, 6 mls (9.5kms) path. Rlwy Stn, Harling Rd. 1.5 mls.

- BB   The Old Dairy, White Hart Street, NR16 2NE. T./F. 717687. www.olddairyharling.co.uk
BB £+++ D1, T2, F1 P/l S/r. Car parking while away, lift to Knettishall £5, (return by train)
- PH BB   Nags Head, Market Street, NR16 2AD. T.718140 BB £+++ D2, T2. S/r. V. Rstr. L & E 7 days
- PH   Swan Inn, T.717951, meals,
- S R   General Store 7am to 9pm, PO, chemist. Fish & chips (not Sun), Chinese take-away (not Tues)

 # New Buckenham (Norwich) Std 01953

- BB   Pump Court, Church Street, NR16 2BA. T.861039 F.861153 www.pump-court.co.uk BB £+++
D1, T1. F1. V, P/l, S/n, D/f, Cyc, P/u, B/d.
- PH   The George, T.860043, meals. The King's Head, T.860487, meals.
- S R   General Store & PO.   Fish & chips - Thursday evening, Saturday lunch.

Thetford Std 01842. 5 miles (8kms) see notes on Transport.

- PH   Black Horse Inn, GR:873832. Norfolk Plover, GR:865827. Red Lion Inn, GR:872830.
- Inn   Anchor Hotel, Bridge Street, IP24 3AE. T.763925 F.766873 BB £++++ D9, F2, T3, S4. V, P/l,
S/r, Dgs, D/f. Rstr & B/m
- H R   Thomas Paine, White Hart Street, IP24 1AA. T.755631. F.766505. www.thomaspainehotel.co.uk
BB £+++ D7, T2, S3. Rstr. 7 days
- H R   Bell Hotel, King Street, IP24 2AZ. T.754455. F.755552. www.bellhotel-thetford.com
£++++ D16, T13, S11, F1 & 5 feature rooms.   Rstr. & B/m 7 days
- H   Wereham House Hotel, 24, White Hart Street, IP24 1AD. T.761956. F.765207.
www.werehamhouse.co.uk   BB £++++ D4, T2, S1, F1.   EM, V, P/l, S/r, D/f, Cyc.
- BB   Mrs. M. Findlay, The Pink Cottage, 43 Magdalen Street, IP24 2PB. T.764564.
maggie.findlay1@btopenworld.com BB £+ T2, S1.   P/l, D/f, Cyc.
- BB   The Old Rectory, 30 Raymond Street, IP24 2EA T.765419.   BB £++ T1, S1, F1. V, Cyc.
- G   The White House, 4 Raymond Street, IP24 2EA. T.754546. F.765055. jumason@btinternet.com
BB £+ D1, T2, S1, F2.   S/r.

Thorpe Woodlands Std 01842   2 miles (3kms) along Peddars Way on River Thet

- C   Small nightly charge: toilet/washroom, no shower, limited shop. Large parties
T.751042 (Forest Enterprises) Easter – September.

West Harling (Norwich) Std 01953

- C   The Dower House Touring Park, East Harling, NR16 2SE. GR:970852. T.717314. F.717843.
www.dowerhouse.co.uk 60 tents. Showers, Shop, Rstr. £8.30-£14.95 per tent. March - October

Bridgham (Norwich) Std 01953 Phone box, no shops.

- PC   Bridgham Heath GR:936871. South side of A11. Car parking. Refreshment stall at times.

East Wretham (Thetford) Std 01953.

- BB   Jan Broughton, Manor Cottages, 4 Church Road, IP24 1PL. GR:919905 T./F.498924 BB £+
D2, S1. P/l, D/f, S/n, Dgs (outside kennel), stabling, Cyc, P/u, B/d. No EM - lift to pub.
- BB   Highfield, Windmill Lane, IP24 1QR T.498700. BB £++ D1, T1, S1, F1. V, S/r, Dgs, Stabling,
Cyc. No EM - lift to pub by arrangement.

Great Hockham (Thetford) Std 01953 1.5 miles (2.4kms)

- PH   The Eagle, Harling Road, T.498216. No food.
- BB   Manor Farm Ventures, Vicarage Road, IP24 1PE GR:951926. T./F.498204. manorfarm@ukf.net
BB £+ /£+++ D1, T/F1, S1. V, P/l, S/n, D/f, Stabling, Cyc, P/u, B/d. No EM - lift to pub.
- C   Puddledock Farm Campsite, IP24 1PA. GR:941925. T.498455. wendy.rands@amserve.com
30 pitches, from £4 per tent. Showers, etc. Dgs. No food.
- S   The Stores.

Thompson (Thetford) Std 01953 1 mile (1.6kms)

- I   The Chequers Inn, Griston Road IP24 1PX. T.483360. F.488092. themcdowalls@barbox.net
BB £++++ D3, V. Dgs. Cyc.   Rstr. & B/m 12.00 to 14.00 18.30 to 21.00

Thompson (Thetford) Std 01953 1 mile (1.6kms) (continued)

BB   Lavender Garnier, College Farm, IP24 1QG. GR:932967. T./F.483318. collegefarm@amserve.net
BB £++ D2, T1. V, P/l, D/f, Cyc. Parking while walkers are away.

BB   Mrs. Brenda Mills, Thatched House, Mill Road, IP24 1PH. GR:918967. T.483577.
thatchedhouse@amserve.com BB £++ D1, T2.   V, P/l, D/f, Dgs, Cyc, S/n, P/u, B/d,

BB C   Mr & Mrs. Hornsey, Lands End, Butters Hall Lane, IP24 1QQ. T./F.488070. BB £+ Riding

 # Great Ellingham (Attleborough) Std 01953

BB   Home Cottage Farm, Penhill Road, NR17 1LS. GR:002955 T.483734. maureenhcf@msn.com
BB £+ Serviced apartment (reductions for larger groups or stays of 2 nights or more)
D1, T1, F1. High tea, V, D/f, S/r, Dgs, Stabling, Cyc, P/u.

 # Mundford (Thetford) Std 01842

BB   Colveston Manor, IP26 5HU. T.878218. F.879218. mail@colveston-manor.co.uk
www.colveston-manor.co.uk BB £+ D2, T1, S1. Stabling, etc. P/u

Stow Bedon (Attleborough) Std. 01953 3 miles (5km)

BB   Home Farm, NR17 1BZ. GR:956962. T.483592. F.488449. ejdoveandson@btconnect.co.uk
BB £++ D1, T1. P/u.

Griston (Nr. Watton, Thetford) Std 01953 3 miles (5km)

PH   Waggon & Horses, Caston Rd, IP25 62D T.883847 Rstr. & B/m L (not Tues + Thurs) E (not Sun)

BB   Mrs. D. Ulrych, Park Farm, Caston Road, IP25 6QD. T.483020 F.483056.
www.parkfarmbreckland.co.uk BB £+ T1, D1. P/u.

BB   Mrs. J. Garner, Hall Farm, (on A1075) IP25 6QF. T.881626 F.883131 £++

Watton (Thetford) Std 01953 ECD Thursday 1 mile (1.6kms)

B   Barclays, NatWest, Lloyds/TSB, Norwich & Peterborough.

H R   Hare & Barrel Hotel, 80, Brandon Road, IP25 6LB GR:905007. T./F.882752. BB £+++
D4, T7, F1, S6. P/l, Cyc. Rstr & B/m - L & E 7 days, www.hare-and-barrel-hotel-norfolk.co.uk

H R   The Willow House, 2, High St, IP25 6AE GR:916008. T.881181. F.885885. www.willowhouse.net
BB £+++/£++++ D3, T3, F1. V, P/l, S/r, D/f, Cyc, P/u. Rstr & B/m - L 7 days, E not Sunday.

H   Crown Hotel, 25, High Street, IP25 6AB. T.882375. BB £+++ S2, T3, D1. Meals.

R BB   Richmond Park Golf Club, Saham Road, IP25 6EA. GR:908012. T.881803. £++

R S   Chinese, Turkish, English take away, Mr. Chips. Somerfield, Tesco Superstore, Londis early-late,

 # Carbrooke (Nr. Watton, Theford) Std 01953

BB   Mrs. Shirley Carr, White Hall, IP25 6SG. GR: 936016. T.885950. whitehallnorfolk@aol.com
BB £++ D2, T1, D/f, S/r, Cyc. P/u, B/d, stabling. No EM, lift to pub (return by taxi).

Saham Toney (Nr. Watton, Theford) Std 01953 2 miles (3kms)

PH   The Bell, Bell Lane, IP25 7HD. GR:903018. T.884934. Meals

H R   Broom Hall Country Hotel, Richmond Rd, IP25 7EX. GR:903012. T.882125. F.885325. BB £++++
www.broomhallhotel.co.uk D9, T3, S1, F2. V, P/l, Dgs, Cyc, S/r. Rstr & B/m - L 7 days, E not Sun

S   Post Office & Stores, Richmond Road. GR: 902019. T.881317

Little Cressingham (Thetford) Std 01953

BB   Sycamore House, IP25 6NE. T./F.881887. BB £++ D2, T1, S1. V, P/l, D/f, Dgs, S/r, Cyc, B/d.
No EM, lift to pub.

Great Cressingham (Thetford) Std 01760

PH   The Windmill Inn, Water End, IP25 6NN GR: 845018. T.756232. Meals

BB   The Vines, The Street, IP25 6NL. GR:849016. T.756303. www.thevines.fsbusiness.co.uk
BB £++ D2, T1., S1. P/l, D/f, S/n, Dgs, Stabling, Cyc. P/u, B/d

Ashill (Thetford) Std 01760

PH   White Hart, Church Street, IP25 7AW. GR: 886043

BB   G.C. Pickering & Son, Moat Farm, Cressingham Road, IP25 7BX. GR:876035. T.440357.
F.441447. BB £+++ D2, T1. (or F) EM, Dgs, Cyc, P/u. B/d

Ashill (Thetford) Std 01760 (continued)

C Spauls Caravan & Camping Park, Brick Kiln Farm, Swaffham Rd, IP25 7BT. GR:875041. T.441300. brick.kiln@onetel.com 30 pitches, Tents from £4.70. Showers, etc. laundry, D/f, Dgs, Stabling & grazing

South Pickenham (Swaffham) Std 01760

PO No shop, Post Office only

North Pickenham (Swaffham) Std 01760

S Shop & PO, open mornings only . Opposite Blue Lion

PH Blue Lion, Hillside, PE378JZ. GR:864069. T.440289. Meals.

BB Riverside House, Meadow Lane, PE37 8LE GR:865065. T.440219. BB £+ D2, T1. V, P/l, D/f, S/r, Cyc, P/u, B/d

Necton/Swaffham Std 01760

S R 100m, west of route crossing A47: Garage shop & Macdonalds

Swaffham Std 01760. 2 mile (3kms) Most things are near the Market Place.

H R George Hotel, Station Street, PE37 7LJ. T.721238. www.bw-georgeswaffham.co.uk BB £++++ D10, T15, S2, F2. V, P/l, S/r, D/f, Dgs, Cyc. Rstr. all day.

H Horse & Groom, 40 Lynn St, PE37 7AX. T.721567. F.725542. BB £++++ D5, T5, S1, F1. Meals, V, Pl, D/f, S/r, Cyc. Quiet enclosed beer garden.

H R Strattons, 4, Ash Close, PE37 7NH. T.723845. F.720458. www.strattons-hotel.co.uk BB £++++ D7, T1.   V, P/l, D/f, Dgs, S/n, Cyc, P/u, B/d.   Rstr.

BB Mrs D. Harvey, Glebe Bungalow, 8a Princes St. PE37 7BP. GR:816089. DoreenMHarvey@aol.com T.722764. BB £+ D1, T1, P/u.

BB Mrs C.Webster, Purbeck House, 46 Whitsands Road. PE37 7BJ. GR:815090. T.721805. BB £+ D2, T2, S2,F2, P/l, D/f, Cyc.

B H.S.B.C., NatWest, Lloyds T.S.B., Norwich & Peterborough, Nationwide.

R Mr Chips, Mother Hubbard's, F.& C., C. Cheng and Hong Kong House Take-Aways.

R Romford House Country Restaurant, The Coffee Shop, T Pot Inn, Pedlars Hall Cafe.

R Market X Restaurant. T. 724260, Village Tandoori,

PH Greyhound. White Hart, Norfolk Hero.

PH Red Lion Motel. T.721022. BB £++ D5, T7.

Taxi J.B. Taxi Service. T.441273. mobile 07801 796007. Advance bookings

C Breckland Meadows Touring Park, Lynn Rd. PE37 7PT GR:809094. www.brecklandmeadows.co.uk T.721246. From £6 per tent. Showers, etc. Up to 45 pitches.   March-October

Sporle (King's Lynn) Std 01760

PH Squirrells Drey, PE32 2DR.   GR:848113. T.724842. B/m, Rstr. Tuesday – Sunday.

S Threeways Stores, The Street. PE32 2DR. GR:849111. T.724300. 6.00 (Sunday 7.30) to 20.00

S Newsagent & General Store. GR:849113. Post Office opposite Threeway Stores.

BB Corfield House, The Street, PE32 2EA. GR:849106. T.723636. www.corfieldhouse.co.uk BB £+++ D2, T2. V, P/l, D/f, Dgs, S/n, Cyc, P/u, B/d.

BB Cambridge Cottage. Love Lane, PE32 2EP. GR:844110. T.723718. BB £ D2, S1. V, Pl, D/f, Dgs, Cyc, P/u.

 # Wendling (Dereham) Std 01362

H R Greenhanks Country Hotel, Swaffham Road, NR19 2AB. T.687742. F.687760 BB £++++ D3. T3. www.greenbankshotel.co.uk EM, V, D/f, Dgs, S/r, Cyc. P/u. Special diets catered for.

 # Gressenhall (Dereham) Std 01362

BB Wood Hill, NR19 2NR. T.699186. F.699291. tania.bullard@btopenworld.com BB £++ D2, T1. P/u

Castle Acre (King's Lynn) Std 01760

I Ostrich Inn, Stocks Green, PE32 2AY GR:818152. T.755398. BB £ June - September D1, F1. ,L. & E. V, P/l, B/d.

Castle Acre (King's Lynn) Std 01760 (continued)

PH   Albert Victor, Stocks Green. PE32 2AE T.756213. Meals, V, Dgs. Beer garden

R S   Castlegate Stores & Restaurant, Stocks Green. Open 7 Days.

BB   Gill Clarke, Gemini House, Pyes Lane, PE32 2XB. T.755375. BB £/£++ D2, T2. V, P/l, D/f, Dgs. S/r, Cyc. Car parking while away.

BB   Alison Loughlin, Old Red Lion, Bailey St, PE32 2AG. T.755557. www.oldredlion.here2stay.org.uk BB £/£++ Group rates neg. D2, T2, F2. Vegetarian wholefood menu only. D/f, Dgs, S/n, Cyc.

BB R   Willow Cottage Tea Room & Bed & Breakfast, Stocks Green, PE32 2AE. T.755551. F.755799 www.broadland.com/willowcottage BB £++ /£+++ D2, T2. V, P/l, S/n, D/f, Cyc, P/u, B/d Tea Room 10.30 - 17.30, 7 days Mid February-November. B & B all year (except Xmas).

BB   Rupert Guinness, 3 Stocks Green, PE32 2AE. T.755564. BB £++ D1, T1, S1. S/n, D/f, Dgs, Cyc.

S PO   Spar Stores & PO Foxes Meadow, PE32 2AS GR:817154. T.755274. Shop 8.00 to 21.00 7 days.

 # Brisley (Dereham) Std 01362

BB   Tully Lodge, School Road, NR20 5LH. T./F.668493. BB £++/£+++ D1, T1. S/n, Cyc, P/u, B/d

PH   Brisley Bell. Meals to be ordered before 20.00

Great Massingham (King's Lynn) Std 01485

S R   Village Store & PO, 12/14 Station Road, PE32 2HY GR:798229. T.520272. 8.00 - 17.30 (Wed 8.00 - 13,00, Sun 9.30 - 12.30) Snacks - take away or garden/seating area available.

Kings Lynn Std 01553. 12 miles (19kms) buses to Swaffham, Massingham & Hunstanton.

Y   Youth Hostel, Thoresby College, College Lane, PE30 1JB. GR:616199. T.0870 770 5902. F./5903. 35 Beds (Open April - September - not every day)

Harpley (King's Lynn) Std 01485

PH   Rose & Crown, Nethergate Street, PE31 6TW. GR:788258. T.520577. Meals (not Mon E)

BB   Mrs. Robert Case, Lower Farm, PE31 6TU. GR:795260. T.520240. BB £+++ D2, T1. P/l, D/f, Cyc, Stabling, Dgs (outside)

Great Bircham (King's Lynn) Std 01485. 1.5 miles (2.4kms)

R S   Bircham Windmill, PE31 6SJ. GR:760326. T.578393. Tearoom, Bakery, Mill. Apr-Sept.10.00-17.00
Cottage   D1, T1 (bunks). self catering, S/n, Dgs, Stabling, Cyc. April - Sept.   www.birchamwindmill.co.uk

H R   Kings Head Hotel, Lynn Road, PE31 6RJ. GR:767322. T.578265. BB £++++ D3, T1, S1, V, P/l, D/f, S/r, Cyc. Rstr. L. & E. 7 days.

S   Country Stores, Lynn Road, PE31 6RJ. T. 578502. Closed Sunday.

PO   Bircham Arts & Crafts, 48 Church Lane, PE31 6QW. T.578203. PO & Gallery.

Sedgeford (Hunstanton) Std 01485

PH   King William IV, Heacham Road, PE36 5LU GR:710366. T.571765. Rstr. & B/m. except Monday (& winter Sunday E.)

BB   Park View, PE36 5LU. GR:711366. T.571352. BB £+, D1, T1, S1. EM, Pl, D/f, S/n, Cyc. Mar- Nov.

S   Shop/PO by village green. 7.30 - 18.30.

Ringstead (Hunstanton) Std 01485

I   Gin Trap, 6 High Street, PE36 5JU GR:706404. T.525264. F.525321 www.gintrapinn.co.uk BB£++++ D2, T1. V, P/l Rstr. & B/m

C   Courtyard Farm, Ringstead. GR:729400. T.525654 F.525211. No regular campsite phone Rose Bowman for permission to camp at farm.

BK   Courtyard Farm Bunkhouse Barn, PE365LQ. GR:729400. T.525251 F.525211. (Rose Bowman) courtyardfarm.organic@virgin.net Booking essential. £6 per night. 12 Bunk Beds, (two rooms) bring bedding and cooking equipment. S/n, Dgs, Stabling, Cyc.

S PO   Ringstead Stores, 41 High Street, PE36 5JU GR:707406. T.525270 . Shop 8.30 - 1730 Sun, Mon, Thurs, Fri. 8.30 - 13.00 Tues, Wed, Sat. P.O. 9.00 - 12.00 Mon, Thurs, Fri. Sat.

Hunstanton Std 01485. 3 miles (5kms) via Ringstead Downs & Lodge Farm. Ecd Thursday

Y   Youth Hostel, 15 Avenue Road, PE36 5BW. GR:674406. T.0870 770 5872 F./5873
  45 beds. Closed November –11th April & Sundays except July & August.

G   The Gables, 28 Austin Street, PE36 6AW. T.532514. www.thegableshunstanton.co.uk
  BB £++ D4, T1, F3. EM, V, P/l, S/n, D/f, Cyc, P/u, B/d.

H R   Mrs. K. Lombari, Sutton House Hotel, 24 Northgate, PE36 6AP T.532552. 6enelli@freeuk.com
  BB £++++ D4, T2, F2, V, P/l, S/r, D/f, Dgs (small), Cyc, P/u, B/d.   Snacks L. Rstr. E.

G   Mr. & Ms. Sturgess, Garganey House, 46 Northgate. PE36 6DR. T.533269.
  sturgess@garganey.fsnet.co.uk BB £+/£++ D3, T1, S2, EM, V, P/l, S/n,

G   Rosamaly Guest House, 14, Glebe Avenue, PE36 6BS. GR:675413. T.534187.
  www.rosamaly..co.uk BB £++ D2, T1, S2, F1, EM, V, P/l, S/n, D/f, Dgs. Cyc.

C   Searles Leisure Resort, South Beach Rd, PE36. GR:671404. T.534211 F.533815 www.searles.co.uk
  289 tent pitches. Showers, laundry, shop, 3 rstrs + fish & chips. £10.23 per night. Feb-Dec

B S R   Barclays, NatWest, Nationwide. Food stores, supermarket. Fish and chips, cafes, restaurants.

Old Hunstanton Std 01485

I   Neptune Inn, 85, Old Hunstanton Road. PE36 6HZ. T.532122. www.neptune-inn.com
  BB £++/£++++ D5, T1, S1, Dgs. Rstr. & B/m L & E

H R   Caley Hall Hotel, Old Hunstanton Rd, PE36 6HH, T.533486. F.533348. www.caleyhallhotel.co.uk
  BB £++++ D/T40, S4, F3. V, P/l, S/r, Dgs. Rstr. & B/m, all day, 7 days   March to December

BB   Mrs Burton, 19 Wodehouse Road, PE36 6JW. T.532380. BB £++, D2, T1. P/l, D/f, Dgs, Cyc.
  Parking while walkers are away.

BB   Lesley Poore, Cobblers Cottage, 3 Wodehouse Road, PE36 6JD. T.534036.
  lesley.cobblerscottage@btinternnet.com BB £+/£+++ D1, T2. March-October.

G   Lakeside, Waterworks Road, PE36 6JE T.533763. BB £+++ D4, T2, S2. EM, V, P/l, S/n, Cyc.

Holme (Hunstanton) Std 01485

PH   White Horse, Kirkgate St, PE36 6LH GR:704435. T.525512. Meals 12.00-1400 & 18.00-21.00.

BB   Seagate House, Beach Road, PE36 6LG. T.525510. BB £++++ D2, T1.

BB   Mary & Robbie Burton, Meadow Springs, 15, Eastgate Road, PE36 6LL. T.525279.
  www.visitwestnorfolk.com BB £+++ D1, T1. V, P/l, S/n, D/f, Cyc, B/d

BB   Mrs Shirley Simeone, Eastgate Cottage, Eastgate Road. PE36 6LL T.525218. BB £++++ T1.
  P/l, S/n, D/f, Cyc.

BB   Mrs. J Reynolds, Meadow View, Eastgate Road, PE36 6LN GR:708432 T.525371.
  www.btinternet.com/~holmenextsea/meadowview.htm. BB £+++ V, S/n, D/f. Cyc. P/u, B/d,
  secure parking while walkers are away.

Thornham (Hunstanton) Std 01485

I   Lifeboat Inn, Ship Lane, PE36 6LT. GR:732435. T.512236. F.512323. www.lifeboatinn.co.uk
  BB £++++ D1, T/D12. V, P/l, S/r, D/f (limited), Dgs.   Rstr, & B/m L & E

PH   The Orange Tree, High St. PE36 6LY. GR:734434. T.512213. F.512424BB D4, S2. B/m.

R   The Old Coach House, High St. T.512229. Pizzas & pasta. Daily from 18.00 L. Friday-Sunday

BB   Mr. M. Wyett, Rushmeadow, Main Road, PE36 6LZ GR:741434 T./F.512372.
  www.rushmeadow.com BB £+++/£++++ D2, T1. S/n.

S R   Post Office, Stores, Bakery & Teashop. Opposite the church. T.512264

Titchwell (King's Lynn) Std 01485

H R   Titchwell Manor Hotel, PE31 8BB. GR:760437. T.210221. www.titchwellmanor.com BB £++++
  D6, T6, S1. F2. V, P/l, S/r, D/f, Dgs. Paddock, Cyc. P/u, B/d,   Rstr. & B/m

H   Briarfields, Main Street, PE31 8BB. GR: 757438 T.210742. F.210933 www.norfolkhotels.co.uk
  BB £++++ D11, T6, F4. EM, V, P/l, S/r, Dgs, Cyc.

BB   Mr. Pinder, 1, Main Road, PE31 8BB. GR:761437. T.210612. BB £+ D1. May – October.

Brancaster (King's Lynn) Std 01485

I   Ship Inn, Main Road, PE31 8AP. GR:772439. T.210333. F.210364. BB £++++ D3, T1.   V, S/n. www.theshipinn-brancaster.co.uk   B/m   12.00 - 14.00 & 18.30 - 21.00

BB   Mrs Townshend, The Old Bakery, PE31 8A .   T.210501. 400m. east of Ship. BB £+++   D2, F1.

BB   The Old Stables, Broad Lane, PE31 8AU T.210774. www.glavenvalley.co.uk BB £+++ / £++++ D2, T1. D/f, S/n, Dgs. Cyc, P/u, B/d.

S   Shops Ecd Wednesday, Sunday. Lunch: 1-2.   GR:772437 & 774439.

Brancaster Staithe (King's Lynn) Std 01485

I   The White Horse, PE31 8BY. GR:800442. T.210262 F.210930 www.whitehorsebrancaster.co.uk BB £++++ D8, T4, S(2), F3. V, P/l, S/r, Dgs. P/u. B/d. Rstr. 12.00 to 14.00 & 18.45 to 21.15

PH   Jolly Sailors, PE31 8BJ GR:795444. T.210314. F.210314 . www.jollysailors.co.uk Rstr & B/m 12.00 to 21.00. Country Walking Magazine - "best walkers' pub in Norfolk & Suffolk".

BB   Mrs. J. Carrington-Smith, Redwings, Orchard Close, PE31 8BN T.210459. BB £+++   T2. P/l, S/r, D/f, Cyc, P/u, B/d.

BB   The Smithy, Main Road, PE31 8BJ (opp. Jolly Sailors). T.210638. BB £++   T1.

BB   Fiona Anderson, Apple Store Cottage, PE31 8BJ (close to Jolly Sailors) T.210331.   BB   D1, T1.

S   The Stores & PO, Main Road. GR:800444. T.210338.   8.30 to 18.00

Burnham Deepdale (King's Lynn) Std 01485

R   Deepdale (as below) PE31 8DD. GR:804441 T.210256. F.210158. www.deepdalefarm.co.uk Café

Y   Deepdale Backpackers. D1, T2, Quad 1, Dorm 4. P/l, S/n, D/f, Cyc.   Bedding supplied & equipped kitchen, laundry room.

Group Y   Deepdale Granary Group Hostel, 18 beds, P/l, S/n, D/f, Cyc. Equipped kitchen, bring bedding.

C   Deepdale Camping, 22 tent pitches, Showers, Laundry, D/f, Dgs, Cyc

S PO   Deepdale Garage. T.210350 Adjacent to hostels & campsite. Shop 7 days.

Burnham Market (King's Lynn) Std 01328 1.5 miles (2.4kms)

B S   NatWest (10.00 - 13.00). Barclays (10.00 - 13.00) PO Various shops.

H   The Railway Inn, Creake Road, PE31 8EN. T.730505.

PH   Lord Nelson, Creake Rd, PE31 8EN. GR:835422. T.738321. www.lordnelsonburnhammarket.co.uk F.738001. BB £+++/£++++ D2, F2. V, P/l Dgs. Rstr. & B/m, L & E

H   Hoste Arms, The Green, PE31 8HD GR:831422. T.738257. F.730103. www.hostearms.co.uk BB £++++ 28 rooms.

BB   Mrs L. Roll, Wood Lodge, Herrings Lane, PE31 8DW. GR:830426. T.730152 F.730158. BB £+++ T2. S/n, Dgs

BB   Holmesdale, Church Walk, PE31 8DH T.738699. www.burnhammarket.co.uk BB £++++   D1, T1. V, P/l, S/n, D/f, Dgs, Cyc, P/u, B/d.

R   Village Tea Room T.738967.   Fishes Restaurant. T.738588, 12.00 - 14.00 + 19.00 - 21.00 Chinese take-away.

Burnham Overy Staithe (King's Lynn) Std 01328

PH   Hero, Wells Road, PE31 8JE. GR:845443. T.738334. Meals.

BB   Mrs. V. Smith, The Brambles, Gong Lane, PE31 8JG. T.730273. F.730831 dsmith6970@aol.com BB £++ /£+++   T2. P/l, S/n, Stabling, Cyc, P/u, B/d.

Holkham (Wells-next-the-Sea) Std 01328 0.5 mile (0.8km)

H   Victoria Hotel, Park Rd, NR23 1RG GR:891440. T.711008. F.711009 www.victoriaatholkham.co.uk BB £++++ D or S9, T1, F2. V, S/r. Rstr. T.713230 12.00 - 14.30, 19.00 - 21.30

R   Ancient House Tea Rooms, NR23 1RG. GR:892440. T.711285.

Wells-next-the-Sea Std 01328

Y   Youth Hostel, Church Plain, NR23 1EQ. GR:917433. T.0870 770 6084. F./6085 31 beds. 16th April - 30th October, 2003

H   Crown, The Buttlands, NR23 1EX. T.710209. F.711432. BB £++++   Meals

H   Edinburgh Hotel, Station Rd, NR23 1AE. GR:918435. T.710210. BB £+/£++++ D1,T1, S1. Meals

Wells-next-the-Sea Std 01328 (continued)

PH   The Bowling Green Inn, Church Street, NR23 1JB. T.710100. Meals

PH   Globe Inn, The Buttlands, NR23 1EU. GR:916434. T.710206. Meals

PH   Ark Royal, Freeman Street and Golden Fleece, The Quay. Meals.

BB   East House, East Quay, NR23 1LE. GR:919437. T.710408. BB £+/£++/£+++ D1, T2. V, D/f, Cyc, P/u, B/d. Closed December

BB   Madeline Rainsford, The Old Custom House, East Quay, NR23 1LD. T.711463. F.710277. www.eastquay.co.uk BB £+++ D2, T1. V, S/n, D/f, Dgs, Cyc.

BB   Mrs J Court, Eastdene, Northfield Lane, NR23 1LH. GR:919436. T.710381. BB £++ D2, T1, V, P/l, S/n, D/f, Dgs, Cyc, P/u, B/d.

G   Kilcoroon, Chancery Lane, NR23 1ER. T.710270. guest@kilcoroon.co.uk BB £+++ D2, T1. V, P/l, S/n, D/f, Cyc. P/u, B/d. 2 night min. stay (one night subject to short notice availability).

BB   Shayes, Meadowside, Two Furlong Hill, NR23 1HQ. GR:913433. T.710470. BB £++ D1, T1. S/n D/f, Cyc.

BB   Wingate, Two Furlong Hill. T.711814. BB £++++ D2, T1. V, S/n, D/f, Cyc.

BB   Brambledene, Warham Road, NR23 1NE. GR:922429. T.711143. BB £+ D2. Nov. to Sept.

BB   Crossways, 2, Park Road. GR:913435. T.711392. www.crossways-bb.co.uk BB £+ D2, T1, F1. EM, V, P/l, S/n, D/f, Cyc.

B   Barclays, 1 High Street. T.755500. Post Office, Station Road.

R   Several cafes, restaurants and fish and chips along the Quay and Freeman Street

C   Pinewoods Holiday Park, Beach Road, NR23 1DR. GR:914453. T.710439. www.pinewoods.co.uk

Café S   Showers, Launderette, Dgs 150 tents. Easter—Decr. Café (incl. breakfast), General store, take away fish/chips pizza 7 days

Warham (Wells-next-the-Sea) Std 01328. 1:3miles (2km)

PH   Three Horseshoes, The Street, NR23 1NL. T.710547. BB £++ D3, S1. V, P/l, S/r, D/f, Dgs, Cyc, P/u, B/d. Rstr. & B/m; L & E.

Stiffkey (Wells-next-the-Sea) Std 01328

C   High Sand Creek, 4 Greenway, NR23 1QF GR:965438. T.830235. F.830119. Showers, laundry. 80 tents. £5.50+ April to October.

S   GR:972442. Seven days a week.

PH   Red Lion, Wells Road, NR23 1QH. T.830552. Meals.

Morston (Holt) Std 01263.

PH   Anchor Inn, NR25 7AA GR:009439. T.741792. Rstr. & B/m, L & E.

BB C   E Hamond, Scaldbeck Cottage, Stiffkey Road, NR25 7BJ. T./F.740188. (daytime T.3740144) eandnhamond@dialstart.net BB £++ D1, T1. V., S/n, D/f, Cyc. February - November. 6 tent pitches, Shower, £7 per person per night.

Blakeney (Holt) Std 01263. Shops and PC at GR:027442.

H   Blakeney Hotel, The Quay, NR25 7NE. T.740797. F.740795 www.blakeney-hotel.co.uk BB £++++. D24, T32, S5, V, Dgs. Rstr. & B/m L & E.

H   White Horse, 4 High Street. NR25 7AL. GR:027442 T.740574 www.blakeneywhitehorse.co.uk F.741303. BB £++++ D6, T1, S2, F1 V. P/l, S/r, Cyc. Rstr.- E (closed Monday), B/m - L & E

PH   King's Arms, Westgate St, NR25 7NQ GR:026440. T.?F.740341. www.blakeneykingsarms.co.uk BB £++++, D4, T1, F2. V, P/l, S/r, D/f, Dgs, Cyc.(limited). Rstr. & B/m, L & E.

S PO   General Store & PO (at King's Arms) shop 8.00 - 22.00 7 days.

BB   Mrs M Image, Peartree Cottage, 81 High Street, NR25 7NA T.741051. BB £+ T1. Summer only.

BB   W & R Millard, White Barn, Back Lane, NR25 7NP (50m from main road) T.741359 http://members.tripod.co.uk/raymillard BB £++/£+++ D2, T1, S1. V, P/l, S/n, Cyc, P/u, B/d.

BB   Navestock, Cley Road, NR25 7NL (opp. church) T./F.740998. john.mander@amserve.com BB £+++/£++++ D1, T1. S/n, D/f, Cyc. Off road parking.

Blakeney (Holt) Std 01263. Shops and PC at GR:027442. (continued)

C   (2 miles south of Blakeney) Long Furlong Cottage Caravan Park, Blakeney Long Lane, NR25 GR:028414. T.740833/740266. Tents. No food. March to October

Wiveton (Holt) Std 01263.1 mile (1.6km) off LDP at Cley

PH   Bell, Blakeney Road, NR25 7TL. GR:042428. T.740101. Meals.

BB   Rosemeade, The Street, NR25 7TH. GR:042432 . T.740747 BB £++ D1, T1

Cley-next-the-Sea (Holt) Std 01263.

H   George Hotel, High Street, NR25 7RN. T.740652. F.741275 www.thegeorgehotelcley.com
BB £++++ D8, T2, F2. V, Dgs. Rstr. & B/m L& E.

Cley-next-the-Sea (Holt) Std 01263

G R   Cookes of Cley, Coast Road. T./F.740776. BB £+++ D4, T2, F2. Rstr. L & E

G   Cley Mill, NR25 7RP. T./F.740209. www.cleymill.co.uk BB £++++ D5, T3. EM, V, S/r, Dgs, Cyc.

PH   Three Swallows, Newgate Green, NR25 7TT GR:047430. T.740526. BB £+++ D4, T/F1.
V, S/r, Dgs, Cyc, B/d. B/m 12.00-14.00 & 18.00-21.00 (12.00-21.00 Fri, Sat. Sun)

BB   The Birches, Holt Road, NR25 7UA T.740534. simon.long@hemscott.net BB £++ D2,
V, S/n, Dgs, Cyc. B/d.

BB   Janet Panton, Droxford, Holt Rd, NR25 7OA. GR:045435. T.740440. BB £++ D1, T1. Apr - Dec

S R   Two shops and teashop in High Street,   P.O. in Holt Road - closed lunch and Tuesdays p.m.

Salthouse (Holt) Std 01263

PH   Dun Cow, NR25 7AJ. GR 075439. T.740467. Meals. 2 self contained flats.

S   PO Stores. GR 075439. Ecd Wednesday, Saturday and Sunday. Closed 13.00 - 14.00

BB   Cumfus Bottom, Purdy Street, NR25 7XA. T.741118. BB £+++ D2, T1. P/l, Dgs, Cyc, B/d

BB   Springholes, Coast Road, NR25 7XG GR:079438. T.740307. BB £++ + D1, D/f, Cyc, S/n

R   Fish & chips

Kelling (Holt) Std 01263

H R   The Pheasant Hotel, Weybourne Road (A149) NR25 7EG. GR:098428. T.588382. F.588101.
www. pheasanthotelnorfolk.co.uk BB £++++ D18, T11, S1. V, P/l, S/r, D/f, Dgs, Cyc.
Rstr & B/m, L. & E.

Kelling Heath (Holt) Std 01263

C   Kelling Heath Holiday Park, NR25 7HW. GR:118415. T.588181. www.kellingheath.co.uk shop,
showers, launderette, Dgs, B/m, pizzas, breakfasts, 285 pitches. mid February - mid December

Weybourne (Holt) Std 01263

H   Maltings Hotel, The Street, NR25 7SY. GR:110432. T.588731. BB 20 rooms, Meals.

PH   Ship Hotel, NR25 7SZ. GR:110430. T.588721. Meals, garden.

BB   The Stables, Bolding Way, NR25 7SW T.588666. www.boldingway.co.uk BB £+++ D2, T1.
S/r, D/f, Dgs, Cyc, B/d. Also available 3 self catering cottages sleeping 2 - 14.

BB   Sheila A Hands, Millpeace, Sheringham Road, NR25 7EY. GR:115431. T.588655. BB £+ D1, T1.
V, S/r, Dgs, Cyc

BB   Mrs. S R Clarke, Sedgemoor, Sheringham Road, NR25 7EY. GR:113429. T.588533. BB £ D2,
V, D/f. Dgs, Cyc.

S   Spar. GR:110431. Ecd Wednesday and Sunday. Closed 13.00 - 14.00

Sheringham Std 01263

Y   Youth Hostel, 1 Cremer's Drift, NR26 8HX. GR:159428. T.0870 770 6024 F./6025
100 beds. Open Fri-Sun 7th Feb-30th Nov, plus most school holidays (incl. half term).

H   The Two Lifeboats Hotel, 2 High Street, NR26 8JR. T.822401. F.823130. BB £++++
D3, T2, F2, S3. All year.

G   Mrs Meakin, Wykeham Guest House, Morley Road North, NR26 8JB. GR:158427. T./F. 823818.
BB £++ D1, T1, S1. April to October. P/l, S/n, Cyc, B/d

Sheringham Std 01263 (continued)

G   The Melrose, 9 Holway Road, NR26 8HN T.823299. www.themelrosesheringham.co.uk
BB £++ D2, T2, S1, F1. V, P/l, S/n, D/f, Dgs, P/u, B/d.

BB   The Birches, 27 Holway Road, NR26 8HW T.823550. patian27@aol.com BB £++ (S £+++) T1, D1.
V, S/n, D/f, Cyc.

BB   Chrissy Foster Worton, Holly Cottage, 14a The Rise, NR26 8QB. GR:162426. T./F.822807.
hollyperks@aol.com BB £++ D2, T1. V, P/l, D/f, Cyc, P/u, B/d. April - Octr. Min. 2 night
stay.

G   Bayleaf Guest House, 10 St Peter's Road. NR26 8QY T.823779. F.820041. bayleafgh@aol.com
BB £+++ D3, T2, F2. P/l. S/n, Dgs (small), Cyc. Bar snacks 16.00 - 21.00

BB   Willow Lodge, 6 Vicarage Road, NR26 8NH. T./F. 822204. www.willow-lodge.co.uk BB £+++
D1, T4, V, S/n, Cyc.

BB   Diana North, Oakleigh, 31, Morris St. NR26 8JY. T.824993. dnorthoak@hotmail.com
BB £+/£++ D1. S1. V, S/n, D/f, Cyc, P/u. April to October.

BB   Mrs. Gray, Elmwood, 6, The Rise, NR26 8QA. GR:161426 T.825454. BB £+ D1, T1.
S/n, D/f, Cyc, P/u, B/d.

BB R   Whelk Coppers, Westcliff, NR26 8LD. T.825771. www.whelkcoppers.co.uk BB £+ D1, F1.
V, P/l, D/f, P/u, B/d. all year. Tearoom June-Octr. + school hols. 7 days 10.00-17.30 (approx).

R   Craske's, High Street and others including fish and chips.

B   Barclays, HSBC, Natwest, Nationwide, etc.

West Runton (Cromer) Std 01263

BB   Corner Cottage, Water Lane, NR27 9QP T.838180. BB £++ D2, T1. P/l. S/n, D/f, Cyc.

G   Mrs K Elliott, Old Barn, Cromer Rd, NR27 9QT T.838285. BB £+++ D5, EM, V, S/n, D/f, Dgs.Cyc.

C   Beeston Regis Caravan Park, Cromer Road, NR27 9NG GR:174432. T.823614. F.823944
www.beestonregis.co.uk showers, laundry, shop, dgs. 70 tents. From £13 per night. Mar-Oct.

G R   Homefield, 48 Cromer Rd, NR27 9AD T.837337. F.870-134-2544 bandb-norfolk@icscotland.net
BB £+++. D2, T2, S1, F1. EM, V, P/l, S/r D/f, Cyc. Rstr. 18.30 -22.30 (closed Monday)

C   Camping & Caravan Club, Holgate Lane, NR27 9NW T.837544. Showers, shop. Tent pitches
flexible. Members £3.80 - £4.15 per night. Non-members £4.90 - £5.30 per night
www.campingandcaravanningclub.co.uk

Aylmerton (Norwich) Std 01263

I   Roman Camp Inn, Holt Road, NR11 8QD. GR:184406. T.838291. F.837071. BB £++++
D7, T8, F1. V, P/l, S/r, Rstr. & B/m, L & E. garden

G   Woodlands Guest House, Holt Road, NR11 8QA. GR:176408. T.837480. BB £+++
D2, T2, S2, F1. V, S/n, Cyc.

East Runton (Cromer) Std 01263

C   Woodhill Park, Cromer Road, NR27 9PX T.512242 F.515326 www.woodhill-park.com Showers,
laundry, shop. 123 pitches. £5 - £7 + £1.50 per person (under 16s £1, dgs £2) March to Oct.

S   Supermarket, butcher, post office.

PH   White Horse, High Street, NR27 9NX. T.519530. ssmith4857@aol.com Rstr. & B/m

PH   Fishing Boat, High Street, NR27 9NX. Meals

R   Berni's Social Club. Music, bar, snacks, fish and chips.

C   Manor Farm Caravan & Camping Site, NR27 9PR. GR:199417. T.512858. www.norfolkcoast.co.uk
showers, laundrette. Easter to end September.

Cromer   Std 01263 Cabell Road is second on the left east of the rail station. Runton Road runs west along
the front. Third on left is Macdonald Road with several guest houses.

BB   Birch House, 34 Cabell Road, NR27 9HX T.512521. www.birchhousenorfolk.co.uk BB £++
D4, T3, S1. V, P/l, S/n, P/u, B/d.

H   Sandcliff Hotel, 37 Runton Road, NR27 9AS. T./F. 512888. www.sandcliffhotel.com BB £+++
D7, T4, S2, F10. EM, V, P/l

Cromer   Std 01263 Cabell Road is second on the left east of the rail station. Runton Road runs west along the front. Third on left is Macdonald Road with several guest houses. (continued)

G   Glendale Guest House, 33 Macdonald Road, NR27 9AP. T.513278. glendalecromer@aol.com BB £+   D2, T1, S2. V, S/n, Dgs.

H   Red Lion Hotel, Brooke Street, NR27 9HD. GR:220423. T.514964. BB £++++.

BB   Cambridge House, East Cliff, Tucker Street. NR27 9HD. GR:220423, T.512085. www.broadland.com/cambridgehousev BB £+++ D1, S1, F4. V, P/l, S/n, D/f, Cyc.

G   Mrs Votier, Morden House, 20 Cliff Avenue, NR27 0AN. GR:221417. T.513396. www.broadland.com/mordenhouse BB £+++ D3, T2, S1. EM, V.

C R   Seacroft Camping Park, Runton Rd, NR27 9NH. GR:206425. T.511722. F.511512 www.seacroftcamping@aol.com 118 pitches. Showers, shop. Easter to October. £10.70 - £17.50 Hillside Restaurant T.512315. Possibly closed mid-week out of season.

B   Barclays, Abbey National, HSBC, Lloyds TSB, Natwest, etc.

Roughton (Norwich) Std 01263 0.5 to 1.5 (0.8 to 2.4km) off the LDP.

PH   New Inn, Norwich Road, NR11 8SJ. GR:219368. T.761389 Meals

S R   Post office stores. GR:220371. Ecd Sunday.   Fish and chips, eat in or take away.

Fellbrigg (Norwich) Std 01263

R   Fellbrigg Hall (National Trust). GR:193395. T.837444. Not open Thursdays & Fridays.

Aldborough (Norwich) Std 01263

R   The Old Red Lion, The Green, NR11 7AA. T.761451. Meals, 12.00-14.00 & 19.00- 21.00

BB   Butterfly Cottage, The Green, NR11 7AA. GR:184343 T.768198. www.butterflycottage.com BB £++ D1, T1, S1. F1 . EM, V, P/l, S/n, D/f, Cyc, P/u, B/d

S   Days Stores (Spar), The Green, NR11 7AA. T.761275   8.00-20.00 Mon-Sat. 10.00-18.00 Sun.

S   Butcher, PO stores, ecd Wednesday, Saturday and Sunday

PH   Black Boys, The Green. T.768086. Meals.

Erpingham (Norwich) Std 01263

I   Alby Horse Shoes Inn, Cromer Road (A140), NR11 7QE. GR:207324. www.albyhorseshoes.co.uk T.761378. BB £++/£+++ D3. V, P/l, S/r, D/f, Cyc. (P/u & B/d - winter only) No children

PO   under 14. Rstr. (handy for campsite below).   PO at petrol station opposite.

C   Little Haven, The Street, NR11 7QD GR:203322. T./F.768959. 24 pitches £10 per tent. March-October. Adults only (16+)

R   The Ark, The Street, NR11 7QB. GR:195322. T.761535.

PH   Spread Eagle, NR11 7QA. GR:191319. T.761591. Meals

Calthorpe (Norwich) Std 01263

I R   Saracen's Head, Wolterton, NR11 7LX GR:171323. T.768909. F.769993 BB £++++ D5, T1. www.saracenshead-norfolk.co.uk V, P/l, S/r, Dgs, Cyc. Rstr & B/m, L. & E.

Blickling (Norwich) Std 01263

I R   Buckinghamshire Arms, NR11 6NF T.732133 www.buckinghamshirearms-norfolk.co.uk GR:176286. BB £++++ D3. V, P/l, Dgs. S/r, Rstr & B/m, L. & E.

R   Blickling Hall House & Gardens (National Trust). 29th March - 2nd November 10.15 am to 5.15 pm. (House from 1 pm only). Closed Mondays, plus Tuesdays (except August). Garden open Winter weekends 11 am -4 pm. Restaurant open with garden. Park open all year.

Aylsham Std 01263 Shops. Most things are near the Market Place.

B   Post Office, Barclays, HSBC, Lloyds TSB, Alliance & Leicester.

R   Full Range - Fish & Chips, Cafes, Restaurants.

PH   Black Boys Inn, Market Place, NR11 6EH. T.732122. meals   Feathers. Unicorn.

BB   Mrs. J Blake, Birchdale, Blickling Road, NR11 6ND. T.734531 www.smoothhound.co.uk/hotels/birchdale   BB £++ D2, T1, S1, F1. V, P/l, S/n, D/f, Cyc.

BB   The Old Manse, 43, Burgh Road, NR11 6AT. T.731283. BB £+ D1, T1. V, S/n, D/f, Cyc.

Aylsham Std 01263 Shops. Most things are near the Market Place. (continued)

BB The Old Pump House, Holman Road, NR11 6BY. T./F.733789.
www.smoothhound.co.uk/hotels/oldpumphouse BB £++ D4, S1, F1. V, P/l, S/n, D/f Dgs.

BB Tim & Janet Bower, Old Mill House, Cawston Road, NR11 6NB GR:185266 T.732118.
timatmill@aol.com BB £++ D1, T1. Cyc.

Banningham (Norwich) Std 01263

BB Poplar Farm. North Walsham Road, NR11 7DS T.732680. g.harvey@tiscali.co.uk BB £++++
D2, T2. V, P/l, S/n, D/f, Cyc, P/u

PH PO Banningham Crown, Colby Road, NR11 7DY. T.733534. F.733082. feneron@msn.com
B/m 12.00-14.30,19-23.30 PO

Felmingham (North Walsham) Std 01692

BB Larks Rise. North Walsham Rd, NR28 0JU. GR:252296 T.403173. www.broadland.com/larksrise
BB £+ D/S/F1 (sleeps 4) , S1. V, P/l, S/r, D/f, Cyc, P/u, B/d. Transport to Banningham for EM

S PO Store & Post Office, Nth. Walsham Rd. GR:250293. T.403340. 7.30-17.30, Sunday 9.00-16.00

North Walsham Std 01692. Various Shops.

H R Kings Arms, Kings Arms Street, NR28 9JX T.403054. F.500095. BB £++++ D2, T3, S2.
V, P/l, S/r, Cyc. Rstr. & B/m 12.00 - 14.00, 19.00-21.00

PH White Swan, 12 Church St, NR28 9DA T./F.402354 B/m 12.00-20.00. Coffee, etc. 11.00-20.00

H R Beechwood Hotel, 20, Cromer Rd. NR28 0HD.T.403231. F.407284, www.beechwood-hotel.co.uk
BB £++++ D15, T2. V, P/l, S/n, D/f, Dgs, Cyc, P/u, B/d. Rstr. E (& Sunday L)

PH Bluebell, Bacton Road.   Black Swan, Black Swan Loke.   Feathers, Orchard Gardens.

BB Chimneys, 51, Cromer Road, NR28 0HB. GR:273306. T.406172. www.chimneysbb.co.uk
BB £++/£+++ D1, T1, F1.

BB Pinetrees, 45, Happisburgh Road, NR28 9HB T./F.404213. www.pinetreesbnb.co.uk BB £++
D1, T1. V, P/l, S/n, D/f, Cyc, P/u. Secure parking while walkers are away.

G Green Ridges, 104 Cromer Road, NR28 0HE. GR:272307 T./F.402448. www.greenridges.com
BB £++ D3, T1, F1. EM £14.99 by arrangement. V, P/l, S/n, D/f, Dgs, Cyc, B/d.

BB Glaven Lodge, 26a, Bacton Road. NR28 9DR. GR:285304. T.404954. www.glaven-lodge.co.uk
BB £+/£++ D2, T1. P/l, S/n, D/f, Cyc.

BB Bradfield House, 19 Station Road, NR28 0DZ T.404352

C Two Mills Touring Park, Yarmouth Rd. NR28 9NA GR:2990287 T./F.405829. www.twomills.co.uk
showers, laundry, shop. 50 pitches. £13.50 (approx.) per night. March to 3rd Jan. Adults only.

B Barclays, HSBC, NatWest, Lloyds TSB, Alliance & Leicester, Norwich & Peterborough.

R English, Chinese, Indian.

North Walsham Std 01692 On alternative route ,south of town at crossing of B1150. GR:278283.

BB The Toll Barn, Heath Road, (Off Norwich Road), NR28 0JB nola@toll-barn.fsbusiness.co.uk
T.403638 F.500993 BB £++/£++++ D1, T1, S1, F1. (self contained lodges optional
continental breakfast £3.50). Nearest EM at Nth. Walsham, approx 1.5 miles

Meeting House Hill Std 01692. Phone box only facility.

Worstead (North Walsham) Std 01692. 1 mile (2km) from Bengate on A149.

PH C New Inn, Church Plain, NR28 9RW GR:302260. T.536296. www.worstead.co.uk/whatson
Bar meals 12.00 - 14.00 & 18.30 - 21.00 (not Sunday evening)   20 tent pitches, £2 per night

G The Ollands, Swanns Yard, NR28 9RP. T./F.535150. www.theollands.co.uk BB £++ D2, T1.
EM, V, P/l, S/r, D/f, Dgs, Cyc, P/u, B/d

G Geoffrey The Dyer House, Church Plain, NR28 9AL T.536562. www.geoffreythedyerhouse.com
BB £++ D1, T1, F1. V, P/l, S/r, D/f, Dgs, Cyc.

G Hall Farm Guest House, Sloley Road, NR28 9RS GR:305251 www.hallfarmguesthouse.co.uk
T./F.536124. BB £++ D1, T1, F1. EM, V, S/r, D/f, Cyc, P/u, B/d

Cottage The Old Chapel, Honing Row, NR28 9RH. GR:303260. T./F. 536005 www.norwichhouse.co.uk/
oldchapel self catering. (100 yds from New Inn) S/n, Cyc, P/u, B/d (3 nights minimum)

Honing Std 01692 Phone box only facility.

East Ruston (Norwich)   Std 01692.

PH   Butchers Arms, Oak Lane. GR:345282. T.650237 Rstr & B/m, L. & E. (large groups catered for)

Stalham (Norwich) Std 01692.

H   Kingfisher Hotel, High Street, NR12 9AN. T.581974. F.582544 kingfisherhotel@hotmail.com
BB £++++ D6, T5, S4, F2. V, P/l, S/r, D/f, Dgs, Cyc. Rstr. & B/m, L & E

PH   Swan Inn, 90 High Street, NR12 9AU. T.581492. Meals L & E

PH   The Maids Head, 110 High Street, NR12 9AU.   The Grebe, 123 High Street, NR12 9BB

BB   Landell, Brick Kiln Lane, Ingham, NR12 9SX. GR:385256. T.582349 www.landell.co.uk
BB £++/£+++   D1, T1, F1.   EM, V, P/l, S/n, D/f, Cyc, P/u.

B S R   Barclays, NatWest, variety of shops. Fish & chips take-away

Stalham Green (Norwich) Std 01692.

PH   The Harnser, The Green, NR12 9QA. GR:382248. T.580347 F.580401 BB+++ T2, V, Cyc.
BB   Meals L & E.

Sutton (Norwich) Std 01692.

H   Sutton Staithe Hotel, NR12 9QS. T.580244. F.583156 www.suttonstaithe.com. BB £++++
D5, T1, S2, F2. V, P/l, Dgs, Cyc. Rstr. & B/m 12.00-14.00 & 18.00-21.30 7 days

S   PO GR:385237. Opposite Garden Centre up cul-de-sac. Ecd Wednesday.

Hickling (Norwich)   Std 01692

I   Greyhound Inn & Berties B & B. The Green, NR12 0YA T.598306. www.greyhoundinn.com
BB £++ £+++ D1, T2, S1. V, P/l, S/r, D/f, Cyc, P/u, B/d. Rstr & snack bar, L. & E.

PH   Pleasure Boat, Staithe Road, NR12 0YW. GR:408225.   T.598211. Meals L & E

BB   Mrs. Meg Froggatt, Paddock Cottage, Staithe Road, NR12 0YJ   T.598259. BB £++ D2, F1.
V, S/n, D/f, Cyc.

S   Hickling Stores. GR:410235. Ecd Wednesday , closed Sunday and 13.00 - 14.00

S   Treasure Box, The Green, NR12 0XN GR410236 . Newsagent, hot & cold drinks available all day.
Monday-Saturday 7.30-18.30, (except Sat. to 17.30) Sunday 8.00-12.30

S   Newsagent & Post Office.

Catfield (Great Yarmouth) Std 01692

BB   Jill Wickens, Grebe Cottage, New Road, NR29 5BQ. GR:388218 T.584179
jill@wickens61.freeserve.co.uk BB £+ D2, T1. S/n, Dgs

PH   The Crown Inn, The Street, NR29 5AZ. T.580128. BB £++   D1, T1. Meals E

Potter Heigham (Great Yarmouth) Std 01692.

BB   Mrs. Molly Playford, Red Roof Farm. Ludham Rd, NR29 5NB T.670604. gplayford@farming.co.uk
BB £+ D2, T1. V, P/l, S/n, D/f, Dgs, Stabling, Cyc, P/u, B/d

S R   Post Office Stores. GR:415190. Shops, Fish & Chip Restaurant. GR:420185.

I   Falgate Inn, Main Road, NR29 5HZ GR:415190. T.670003. BB £/£+++ D2, T2, S1, F1, .
V, P/l, S/r, D/f, Cyc, P/u, B/d.   Rstr. & B/m, L & E.

PH   Broads Haven Tavern, Bridge Rd. NR29 5JD T.670329 F.670729 Rstr. & B/m L & E

Bastwick Repps with Bastwick (Great Yarmouth) Std 01692.

G   Mrs. J. Pratt, Grove Farm, Tower Road, NR29 5JN. GR:427177. T.670205

S   Post Office. GR:423178. Ecd Saturday, closed Sunday. Garage, Spar, Off-licence.

C   Whitehouse Camping, Main Rd, NR29 5JH GR:424180. T.670403. Showers.   20-25 tents. £7

Repps Repps with Bastwick (Great Yarmouth) Std 01692.

C   Willowcroft Camping & Caravan Park, Staithe Road, NR29 5JU. GR:414173. T./F.670380.
www.willowcroft4.freeserve.co.uk 25 tent pitches. Showers £8.50 per night. Most of year.